Consumers' mortgage shopping experience

A first look at results from the National Survey of Mortgage Borrowers

Consumer Financial
Protection Bureau

January 2015

Table of contents

Preface

In the wake of the Great Recession, Congress created the Consumer Financial Protection Bureau (CFPB or Bureau) to protect consumers and help avoid any repeat of the conditions that had led to the financial crisis. It has been widely recognized that dramatic deterioration in underwriting standards led to severe dislocations in the mortgage market, which were transmitted through various mechanisms, including mortgage securitization, into extensive damage to the broader economy. In accordance with the direction laid out by Congress, addressing the mortgage market was a high priority for the Bureau and, in January 2013, the CFPB finalized several mortgage rules, most of which took effect in January 2014. Among these rules, the Ability-to-Repay (ATR) rule requires that lenders generally make a reasonable, good-faith determination that prospective borrowers have the ability to repay their loans. The mortgage servicing rules establish strong protections for homeowners, including those facing foreclosure.

Many of the risky practices that led to the crisis were not present in the market when the ATR rule went into effect, so the Bureau did not anticipate that our rules would affect the broader market in an intense or abrupt fashion. Rather, the point of the rule is to establish important guardrails that will prevent a return to these risky lending practices as memories of the crisis may fade over time.

In the years following the recession, conditions in the mortgage market have, for the most part, slowly and steadily improved, and signals suggest that this should continue in the years ahead.

FIGURE 1   FORECLOSURE AND DELINQUENCY RATES, PERCENT OF ACTIVE LOANS, 2005 – 2014.[1]

■ In Foreclosure   ■ 90+ Days Past Due   ■ 60-89 Days Past Due

Foreclosure rates spiked during the crisis, with millions of people across the country losing their homes. The proportion of homes that were delinquent or in the foreclosure process peaked in late 2009 and has declined steadily since then. It has now fallen to a level not seen since 2008.

FIGURE 2   CASE-SHILLER HOME PRICE INDICES, NATIONAL COMPOSITE AND SELECT CITIES, CHANGE IN INDEX VALUE COMPARED TO SEPTEMBER 2000, 2000-2014.[2]

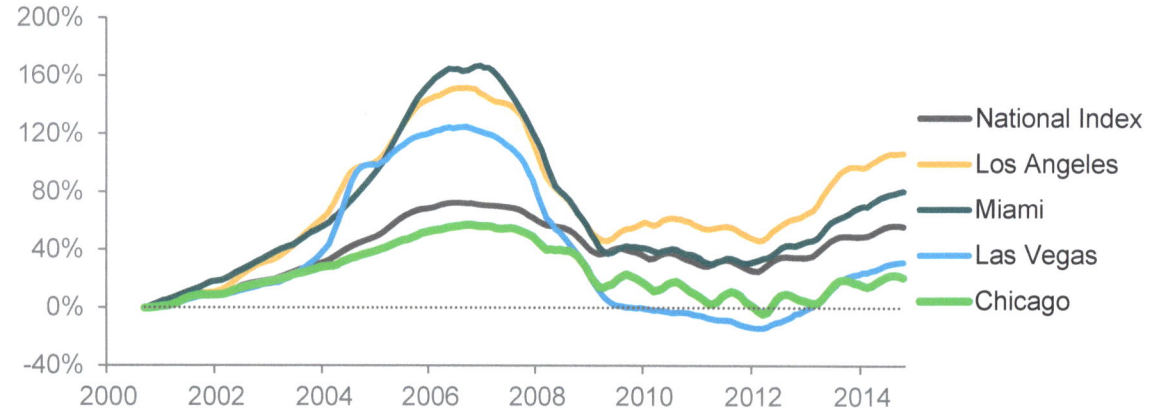

Home prices rose to unprecedented levels in the run-up to the crisis and then collapsed sharply during the crisis. Prices have begun to recover again in the wake of the crisis, as the chart

[1] Mortgage Bankers Association (MBA) National Delinquency Survey

[2] S&P/Case-Shiller

indicates, though it also shows that price appreciation has not been consistent across all markets during this period. The reduction in the "shadow inventory" – homes in or subject to foreclosure – has contributed to this trend of rising home prices. While prices in many cities remain below their all-time high, the price appreciation has reduced the number of borrowers who are "underwater," meaning they owe more on their mortgage than their home is worth. The number of homes that are "underwater" peaked around early 2012, and various estimates agree that over 6 million homes have emerged from negative equity positions since then.[3]

FIGURE 3   NEW AND EXISTING HOME SALES, CHANGE IN SEASONALLY ADJUSTED ANNUAL RATE COMPARED TO JANUARY 2000, 2000-2014.[4]

New and existing homes sales both began declining in 2005 and, after a long slide, both measures have climbed since. Existing home sales have now returned to the level they attained during the years preceding the bubble. New home sales, however, while generally rising since 2011, remain substantially below their pre-bubble levels. Many observers have noted that the recovery of the housing market has been slow over the past several years, perhaps reflecting the continuing effects of the profound dislocations that occurred in the market around the time of the financial crisis and the leading role they played in bringing about the Great Recession.

[3] CoreLogic and Zillow.com.

[4] US Census Bureau and National Association of Realtors (NAR).

Meanwhile, mortgage interest rates remain near historically low levels, aiding affordability for new home purchasers and enabling many existing homeowners to reduce their housing costs. Rates were below 4 percent for much of 2012 and the first half of 2013, prompting a strong wave of refinances. Rates increased in the first half of 2013, which had a substantial negative effect on the refinance market that was felt almost immediately. Rates dipped below 4 percent again in late 2014, though the refinancing market has been slow to recover its prior pace or momentum.

As for the more specific effect of the new mortgage rules on the current market, the data remain scarce given that the effect of the rules was limited to new applications after January 2014, and especially given the multitude of complex factors that dictate conditions in the housing and mortgage markets. In the notes of its Open Market Committee from June 2014, the Federal Reserve presented an insightful and succinct summary of those cross-cutting factors "that might be contributing to a temporary delay in the housing recovery," as follows: "Despite attractive mortgage rates, housing demand was seen as being dampened by such factors as restrictive credit conditions, particularly for households with low credit scores; high down payments; or low demand among young homebuyers, due in part to the burden of student loan debt. Others noted supply constraints, pointing to shortage of lots, low inventories of desirable homes for sale, an overhang of homes associated with foreclosures or seriously delinquent mortgages, or rising construction costs. Several other participants suggested the possibility that more persistent structural changes in housing demand associated with an aging population and

---

[5] Freddie Mac, Primary Mortgage Market Survey.

evolving lifestyle preferences were boosting demand for multifamily units at the expense of single-family homes."[6] Economists and policymakers continue to scrutinize these various influences as they seek to assess the likely further evolution of the housing and mortgage markets going forward.

Given the slow but persistent recovery in many U.S. economic indicators, such as improvements in the unemployment rate, there are reasons to believe that there will be increasing demand from potential first-time homebuyers. Results from the National Housing Survey conducted by Fannie Mae indicate that the majority of young renters (under age 40) still aspire to homeownership for both lifestyle and financial reasons, suggesting that younger consumers are delaying homeownership, not opting out of it.[7] This survey also finds that the most common barriers to homeownership include the inability to afford the down payment or closing costs; insufficient credit score or credit history; and insufficient income for monthly payments. As the economy improves and underwriting loosens, these barriers should become more surmountable and more consumers will likely opt to become homeowners. In this regard, it is notable that recent research reaffirms that even through the most difficult period in the housing market in recent history, "homeownership continues to be a significant source of household wealth, and remains particularly important for lower-income and minority households" that maintain sustainable homeownership over time, largely because of the "forced savings" component of monthly mortgage payments.[8]

As consumers enter the market, the Bureau's Ability-to-Repay rule will ensure that they are only offered mortgages that they can likely afford. With these guardrails now in place, the Bureau is directing attention at ways to empower consumers to select a mortgage that is a good fit for their personal needs and budget. Shopping is important not only to help borrowers understand the different product features available, such as adjustable-rate versus fixed-rate, but also the price

---

[6] Federal Reserve Board, Minutes of the Federal Open Market Committee, June 17-18, 2014, at 8.

[7] "Fannie Mae National Housing Survey: What Younger Renters Want and the Financial Constraints They See." May 2014. www.fanniemae.com/resources/file/research/housingsurvey/pdf/nhsmay2014presentation.pdf

[8] Christopher E. Herbert, Daniel T. McCue, and Rocio Sanchez-Moyano, Is Homeownership Still an Effective Means of Building Wealth for Low-Income and Minority Households? (Was It Ever?), Joint Center for Housing Studies, Harvard University, Sept. 2013, at 48.

at which those products are offered (including the prices of ancillary services, like settlement services or title insurance).

The interest rate on a mortgage is one of the key components of the mortgage's total cost, and mortgage interest rates can vary considerably across lenders, implying that consumers can potentially save a significant amount of money if they shop effectively. Data on daily mortgage rate quotes indicates that the range of interest rates available to a borrower can be significant, even after accounting for loan size and mortgage type.[9] For example, rates can span more than 50 basis points for a conventional mortgage for borrowers with a 760 FICO score and 20 percent down payment. Such a difference can have significant implications. For a borrower taking out a 30-year fixed-rate loan for $200,000, getting an interest rate of 4% instead of 4.5% translates into almost $60 in savings per month. Over the first five years, the borrower would save about $3,500 in mortgage payments. In addition, the lower interest rate means that the borrower would pay off an additional $1,400 in principal in the first five years, even while making lower payments.

Recognizing the potential benefits of effective shopping, the CFPB aims to help consumers become better and more informed shoppers. With that in mind, we are improving mortgage disclosures under the Truth in Lending Act and the Real Estate Settlement Procedures Act. These new "Know Before You Owe" forms will go into effect in August 2015. To support that effort and encourage a culture of mortgage shopping, the Bureau is launching tools that help consumers make more informed decisions and be more effective advocates for themselves as they navigate the mortgage process. It is also conducting a pilot program to explore potential ways to improve the closing process.

Part of this broad effort involves developing a better understanding of how consumers shop for mortgages and how shopping activities affect outcomes, such as the interest rate paid and whether borrowers are able to successfully repay the mortgage. A key part of this is a new data collection called the National Survey of Mortgage Borrowers (NSMB), conducted jointly with the Federal Housing Finance Agency, which is the focus of this report.

---

[9] CFPB analysis of data from Informa Research Services.

1. Survey overview and key findings

This report provides a first look at results from the National Survey of Mortgage Borrowers (NSMB), and examines information related to consumers' mortgage shopping experience. The NSMB is being jointly funded and developed by the Bureau and the Federal Housing Finance Agency to better understand how mortgage markets are functioning for American consumers.[10] The NSMB is a voluntary survey mailed each quarter to a nationally representative sample of consumers who have recently taken out new mortgages. Their identities are never disclosed to anyone at either agency. The survey responses will allow policymakers to learn directly from consumers about their mortgage experiences.

These surveys asked approximately 100 questions covering the entire mortgage process, from when the consumer first started shopping for a mortgage through closing. These questions also asked about consumers' knowledge of the mortgage process, their expectations for the future, recent life events, and demographic characteristics. The first round of the NSMB commenced in early 2014. Surveys were mailed to about 15,000 consumers who had taken out new mortgages during 2013 and over 5,000 respondents replied. The responses to this initial survey will be used as a baseline for comparison with surveys mailed in later quarters, thus allowing policymakers to better track mortgage market developments.

As part of the Bureau's work to expand consumers' ability to shop effectively, the Bureau analyzed a subset of the questions to better understand the mortgage shopping experience for borrowers who had purchased a home in 2013, based on a preliminary analysis of the responses received to the first round of the NSMB. Our focus is on what the data tell us about the early

---

[10] The NSMB draws upon a broader data initiative called the National Mortgage Database (NMDB).

stages of getting a mortgage, particularly the extent to which consumers shopped for mortgages, their knowledge of the mortgage process when they began, and the sources of information they relied on. In this report, we restrict our analysis to respondents who took out mortgages to purchase a home, as opposed to those who were refinancing an existing mortgage who are likely to have different shopping goals and challenges. In total, there were 1,922 respondents who took out a mortgage for a purchase. We pay particular attention to first-time homebuyers and other mortgage borrowers who may have been less knowledgeable about the mortgage process before taking out their mortgage.

Key findings include:

a. Almost half of consumers who take out a mortgage for home purchase fail to shop prior to application; that is, they seriously consider only a single lender or mortgage broker before choosing where to apply. The tendency to shop is somewhat higher among first-time homebuyers.

b. The primary source of information relied on by mortgage borrowers is their lender or broker, followed by a real estate agent. Fewer consumers obtain information from outside sources, such as websites, financial and housing counselors, or personal acquaintances (such as friends, relatives, or coworkers).

c. Most consumers report being "very familiar" with the types of mortgages, available interest rates, and the process of taking out a mortgage. Those who are unfamiliar with the mortgage process are less likely to shop and more likely to rely on real estate agents or personal acquaintances.

d. A sizeable share of borrowers report that factors not directly related to mortgage cost, including the lender or broker's reputation and geographic proximity, are very important in their decision making. Borrowers who express such preferences are much less likely to shop.

2. How much do consumers shop?

The interest rates available for mortgages often vary across lenders, even for the same consumer and for loans with otherwise identical product features. As a result, consumers may save substantial sums if they consider the product offerings of multiple lenders or brokers.

In considering the available options, consumers can shop for a mortgage either before applying for a loan or afterwards (or both). The NSMB asks recent mortgage borrowers about their shopping behavior both before and after their first mortgage application. In this chapter, we discuss what the responses indicate about the amount of comparison shopping consumers engaged in before and after their first application.

The results for pre-application mortgage shopping are shown in Figure 5. Almost half of consumers who took out a home purchase mortgage reported that they seriously considered only a single lender or mortgage broker before applying for a loan. First-time homeowners were only slightly more likely to shop, despite their relative inexperience.

For most borrowers, the mortgage shopping process stops after their first application. As shown in Figure 6, about 77 percent of borrowers applied to only one lender.

The consumers who applied to multiple lenders may have had different motivations. The NSMB asked consumers who applied to multiple lenders about different factors that may have motivated them. These factors are tabulated in Figure 7.

FIGURE 5 HOW MANY DIFFERENT LENDERS/BROKERS DID YOU SERIOUSLY CONSIDER BEFORE CHOOSING WHERE TO APPLY FOR YOUR MORTGAGE?

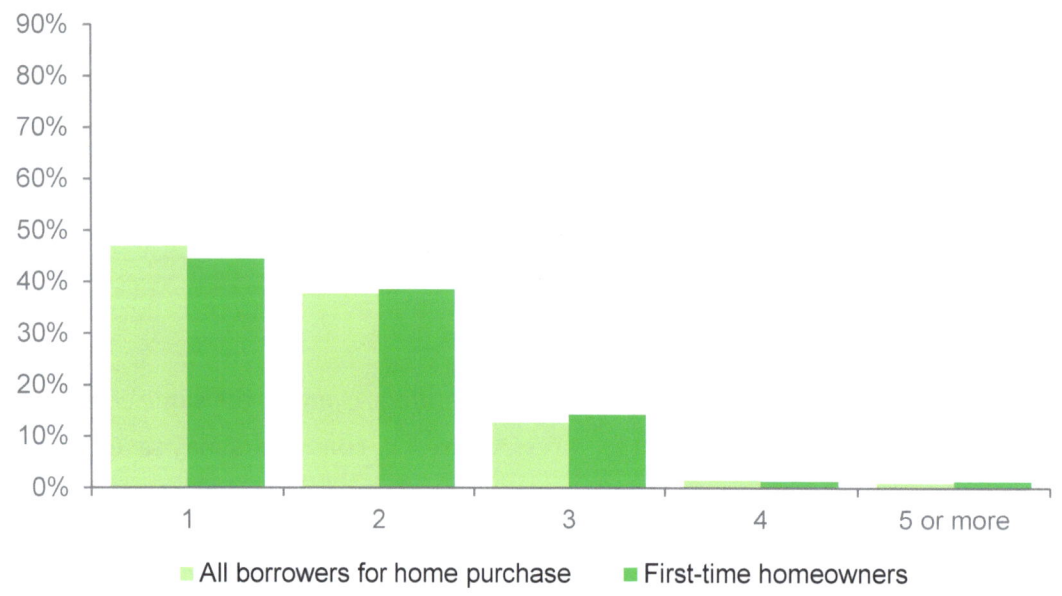

■ All borrowers for home purchase   ■ First-time homeowners

FIGURE 6 HOW MANY DIFFERENT LENDERS/BROKERS DID YOU END UP APPLYING TO?

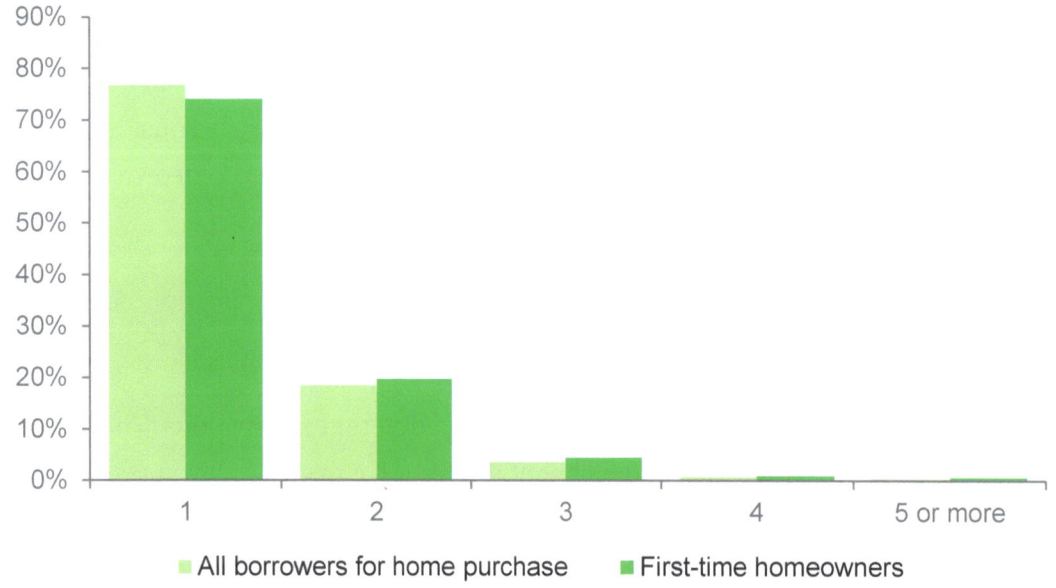

■ All borrowers for home purchase   ■ First-time homeowners

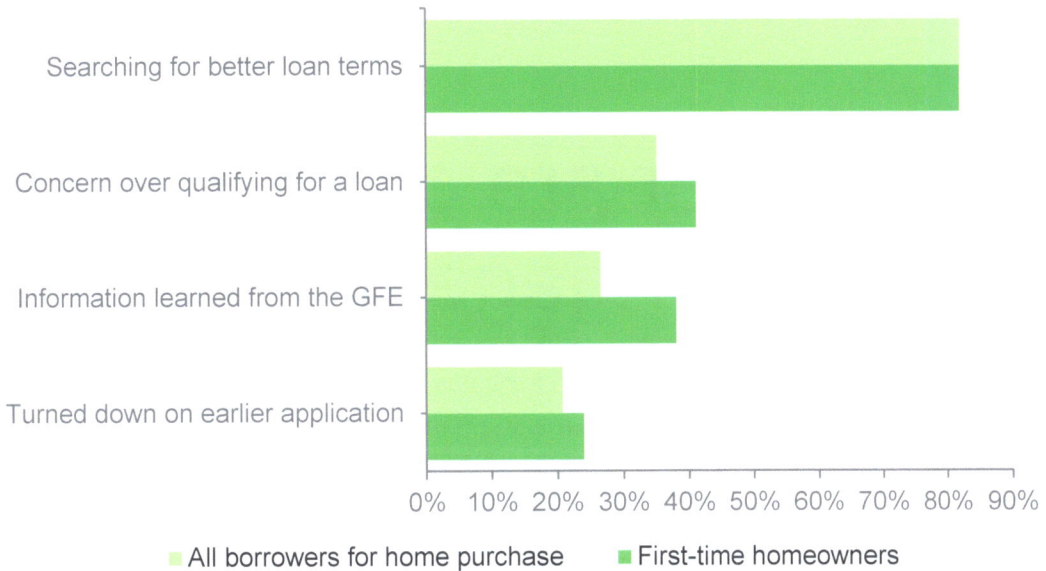

Almost one in five of the borrowers who applied to multiple lenders (comprising about 5 percent of all home purchase borrowers) reported doing so because they had been turned down on an earlier application. Additionally, about 35 percent of borrowers who applied to multiple lenders report being motivated by concerns over whether they would qualify for loan, suggesting that they may have applied to multiple lenders simultaneously. Most borrowers, however, (about 80 percent) applied to multiple lenders out of a desire to find better loan terms.

To some extent, the responses to these questions may understate the amount of shopping activity mortgage borrowers engage in. For example, borrowers may have been able to compare the terms of multiple lenders or brokers without "seriously considering" them as options (although for consumers to obtain a customized rate quote from a lender for comparison purposes the consumer must share a significant amount of information with the lender). Additionally, some borrowers may have seriously considered additional lenders after their first application without filling out a second application. Nevertheless, we believe that these results indicate that a significant minority of consumers may not be shopping enough to ensure they are receiving the mortgage that best fits their circumstances.

In the remainder of this report, we discuss responses to other questions in the NSMB that shed light on the types of borrowers who shop (either before or after application) and the factors that may affect the amount or type of shopping mortgage borrowers do.

3. How familiar are consumers with the mortgage process?

One factor that may affect whether consumers shop for loans is the amount of knowledge they have or believe they have about mortgage loan features and about the process of taking out a mortgage. The relationship between knowledge and shopping behavior is not necessarily clear. On the one hand, less knowledgeable consumers may shop more in an effort to better educate themselves about the range of options available and to ensure that the offers they receive are competitive. On the other hand, less knowledgeable consumers may have more difficulty acquiring or understanding the information available (for example, they may not know the right questions to ask or may find it difficult to evaluate tradeoffs between a lower interest rate for higher upfront fees or costs) and therefore engage in less effort to collect it. In this section, we analyze mortgage borrowers' self-assessments of their knowledge of the mortgage process and how this relates to their shopping activities.

The NSMB asked recent mortgage borrowers to recall the beginning of their mortgage experience and evaluate how familiar they were at the time with various aspects of the mortgage process, including the types of mortgages available, the prevailing interest rates, their own credit history, the money needed at closing, and the income and down payment requirements. In each case, consumers were asked to report whether they had been very, somewhat, or not at all familiar with that aspect of the process. Panel A of Figure 8 shows the results reported by consumers who took out a mortgage for home purchase in 2013. Panel B shows the responses for first-time homebuyers, whom, because of their inexperience, we would expect to be less familiar with the various parts of the mortgage process.

Most consumers (51 percent) said they were "very familiar" with the mortgage process from the beginning, while only 14 percent reported being "not at all familiar" with the process. While the level of familiarity differed somewhat across the parts of the process that borrowers were asked about, similar patterns were observed with about half of consumers or more being very familiar with that part of the mortgage process and 10 percent or fewer being completely unfamiliar. Consumers reported being most familiar with their own credit score and credit history, which may not be surprising given that this is information about themselves and not market offerings. They were least familiar with the money needed for closing, with only 49 percent reporting being very familiar and 14 percent reporting being completely unfamiliar.

As expected, first-time homebuyers report being less familiar with the mortgage process. One in four first-time homebuyers report being completely unfamiliar with the mortgage process from the start and only about a third of these consumers say they were very familiar with the process. The lack of familiarity of first-time homebuyers (relative to experienced homebuyers) was observed across the different parts of the mortgage process. These are all very important aspects of the mortgage process, and a lack of familiarity could hinder a first-time homeowner's ability to make optimal choices.

Panel A: All borrowers for home purchase

Panel B: First-time homeowners

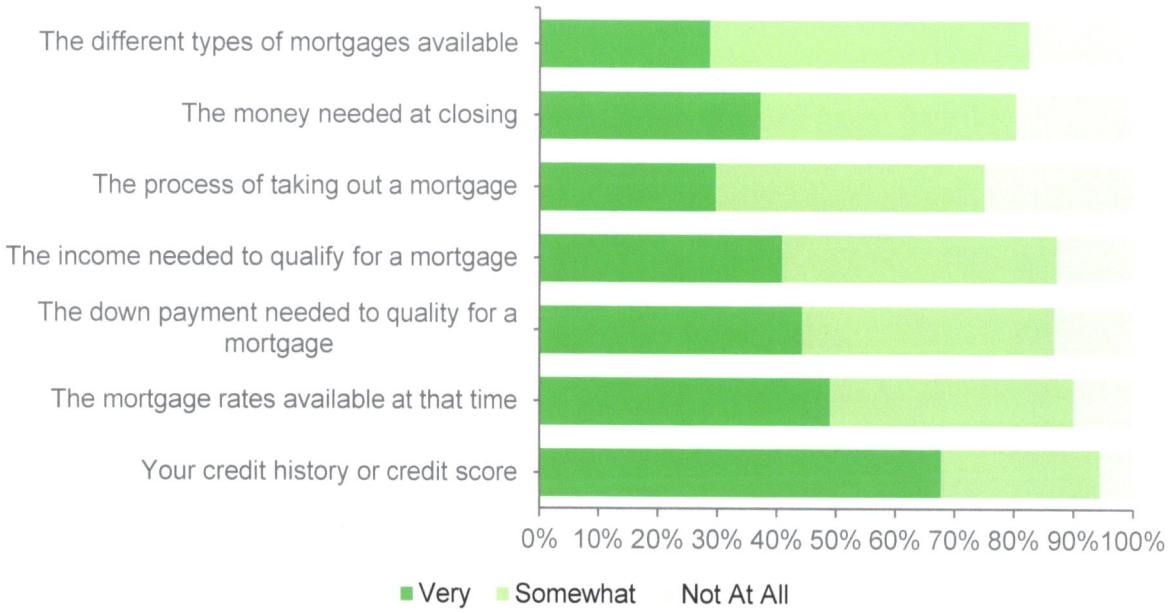

As mentioned earlier, the relationship between consumer knowledge and shopping is not necessarily obvious. Consumers who are more knowledgeable may be more or less likely to shop than consumers with less knowledge or experience. To shed some light on how familiarity with the mortgage process affects shopping behavior, we calculate the share of consumers whom we classify as "shoppers" (defined as consumers who seriously considered more than one lender or broker, as in Figure 5) among consumers who said they were very familiar or not at all familiar with a particular aspect of a mortgage process. The results are shown on Figure 9.

FIGURE 9 PERCENTAGE OF CONSUMERS WHO SHOPPED, AMONG ALL CONSUMERS WHO SAID "VERY FAMILIAR" OR THOSE WHO SAID "NOT AT ALL" FAMILIAR BY ASPECT OF THE MORTGAGE PROCESS,

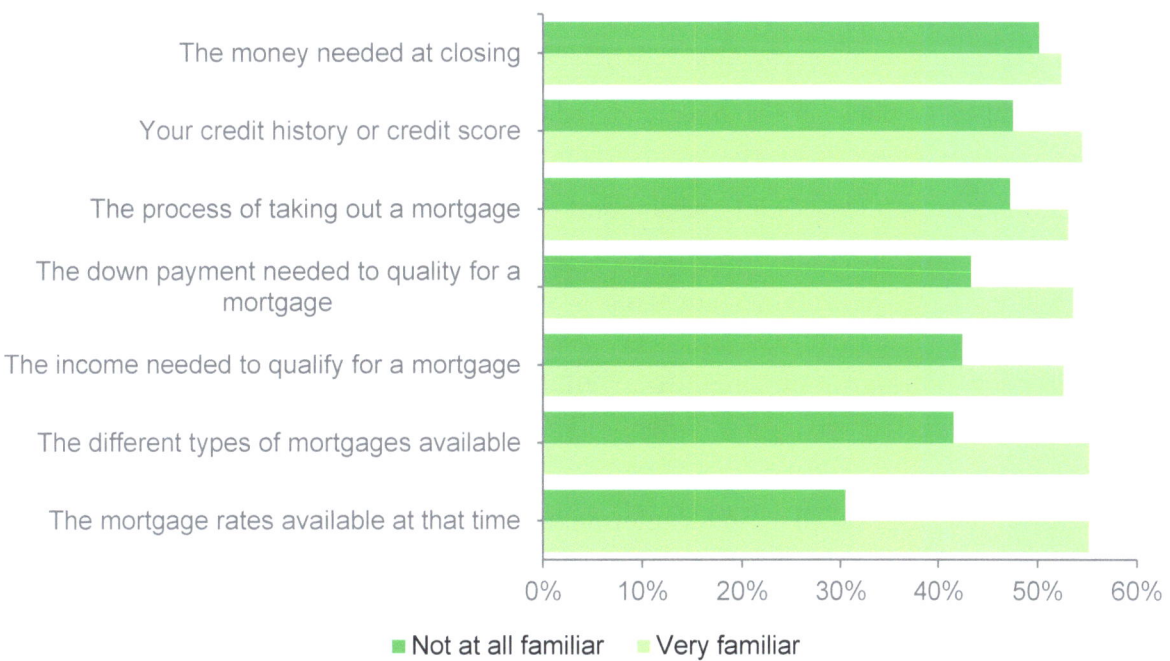

Consumers who report being unfamiliar with some aspect of the mortgage process are less likely to shop, compared to consumers who are very familiar with that aspect. In some instances, the difference in shopping activity is substantial. For instance, consumers who are confident about their knowledge of available interest rates were almost twice as likely to shop as consumers who were unfamiliar with available interest rates. These results support the hypothesis that a lack of knowledge inhibits shopping (presumably, because it makes shopping more intimidating).

4. What information sources about mortgages do consumers use?

So far, we have considered shopping for a mortgage in the narrow sense of considering multiple lenders. Mortgage shopping can also be considered to encompass a wider array of activities related to the collection of information necessary for making a well-informed mortgage choice. To take this more general view, NSMB asks recent mortgage borrowers whether they utilized each of several different information sources. Respondents were asked to report whether they used each source "a lot," "a little," or "not at all."

As shown in Panel A of Figure 10, the source of information that was most commonly used by mortgage borrowers is the borrower's lender or mortgage broker: 70 percent of borrowers for home purchase report using that source "a lot." Real estate agents, who help consumers find a house, are also frequently relied upon for information about mortgages, though only 33 percent of consumers say they used this source a lot.

Other sources of information are used less frequently. Websites that provide information about getting a mortgage were the most commonly used of these sources, though only 20 percent of mortgage borrowers report using them a lot. Even less frequently used were personal acquaintances (i.e., friends, relatives, or coworkers), bankers, or financial planners. First-time homebuyers, as shown in Panel B, are more likely to rely on personal acquaintances and slightly more likely to rely on websites. In other respects, the use of information sources by first-time homebuyers was similar to that of all mortgage borrowers.

FIGURE 10 HOW MUCH DID YOU USE EACH OF THE FOLLOWING SOURCES TO GET INFORMATION ABOUT MORTGAGES OR MORTGAGE LENDERS?

Panel A: All borrowers for home purchase

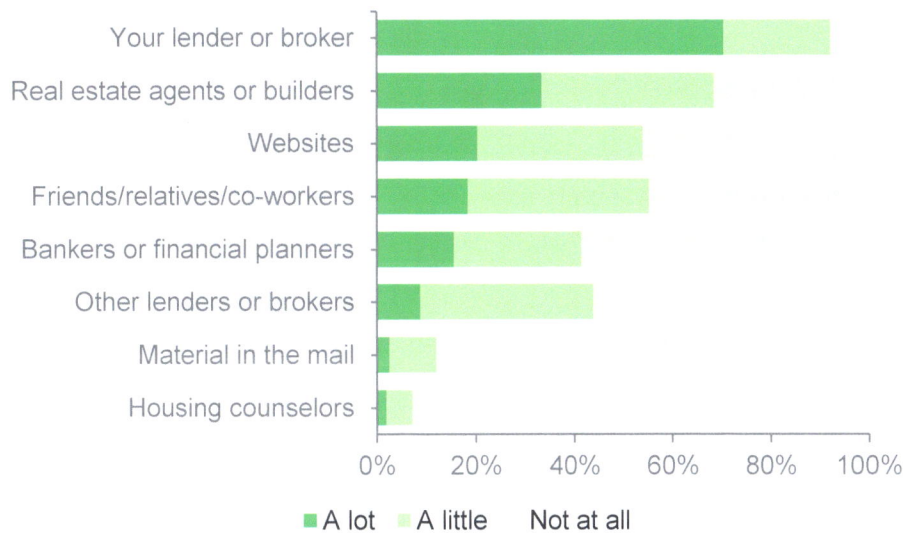

Panel B: First-time homeowners

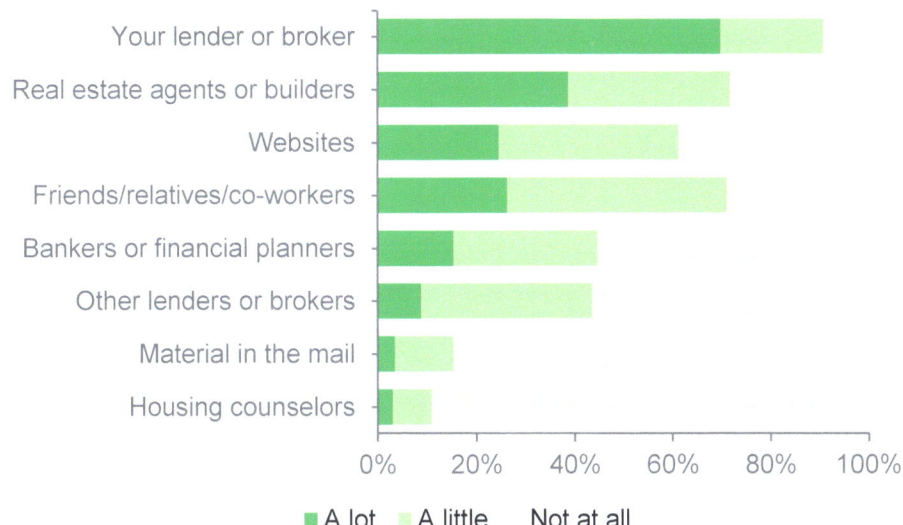

Our earlier results suggest that consumers who are less familiar with the mortgage process are less likely to shop. For these consumers, gathering information about the mortgage process is likely to be particularly important and understanding the sources of information they use may be useful in helping these consumers become more knowledgeable shoppers. Figure 11 compares the information sources used by consumers who reported being "very familiar" with the mortgage process to the information sources used by borrowers who were "not at all familiar" with the process. The results suggest that borrowers used the different sources of information with similar intensities regardless of whether they were informed with the mortgage process, with two notable exceptions. Uninformed consumers tended to rely on personal acquaintances and real estate agents much more than consumers who were very familiar with the process. For instance, while only 11 percent of informed consumers relied on personal acquaintances, this share rises to 36 percent among uninformed ones. A potential explanation is that friends and real estate agents may be better able to convey information in a way that is more accessible to these borrowers.

FIGURE 11 PERCENTAGE OF BORROWERS WHO INDICATED "USED IT A LOT," BY INFORMATION SOURCE, AND BY FAMILIARITY WITH THE PROCESS OF TAKING OUT A MORTGAGE

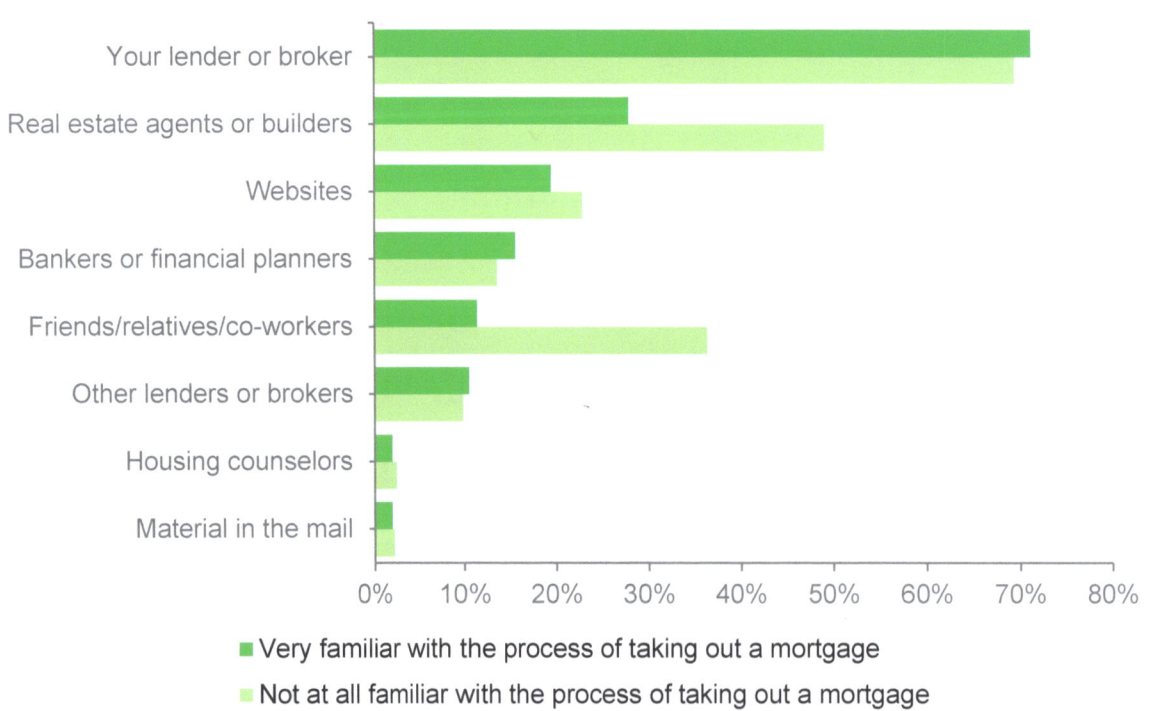

For all home purchase borrowers, we have found that consumers rely heavily on lenders and brokers as a source of information about mortgages. The following question further underscores the important role that lenders and brokers play in helping determine the type of mortgage the consumer chooses. On Figure 12, we find that as many as 70 percent of borrowers for home purchase choose their lender or broker before deciding on the type of loan (we found no difference among first-time homeowners).

FIGURE 12 WHICH OF THE FOLLOWING BEST DESCRIBES YOUR SHOPPING PROCESS? ALL BORROWERS FOR HOME PURCHASE

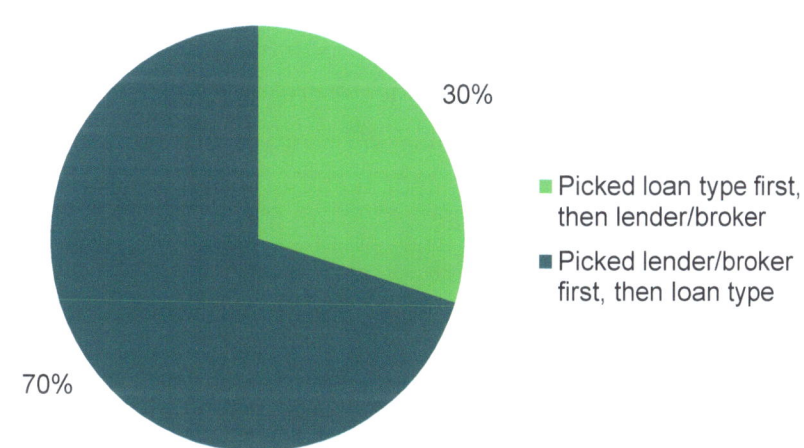

30%

70%

■ Picked loan type first, then lender/broker

■ Picked lender/broker first, then loan type

5. What do consumers look for in a lender or broker?

For some mortgage borrowers, characteristics besides interest rates or other mortgage terms may play an important role in their choice of lender or broker. The NSMB asks borrowers about 11 characteristics of lenders or brokers. For each characteristic, the borrower was asked whether that characteristic was "very," "somewhat" or "not at all" important in their selection. Figure 13 tabulates the responses for each characteristic.

While none of these characteristics were considered very important by a majority of borrowers, three characteristics were very important for a sizeable minority of consumers. Among these is having an established banking relationship with the lender, which was considered to be very important by 42 percent of mortgage borrowers. Since most potential borrowers likely maintain few banking relationships, such a preference could inhibit the number of potential alternative lenders that a borrower considers. A local office nearby is very important for 40 percent of borrowers. Reputation of the lender is very important for 41 percent of borrowers.

FIGURE 13 HOW IMPORTANT IS EACH OF THE FOLLOWING IN CHOOSING THE LENDER/BROKER YOU USED FOR THE MORTGAGE YOU TOOK OUT?

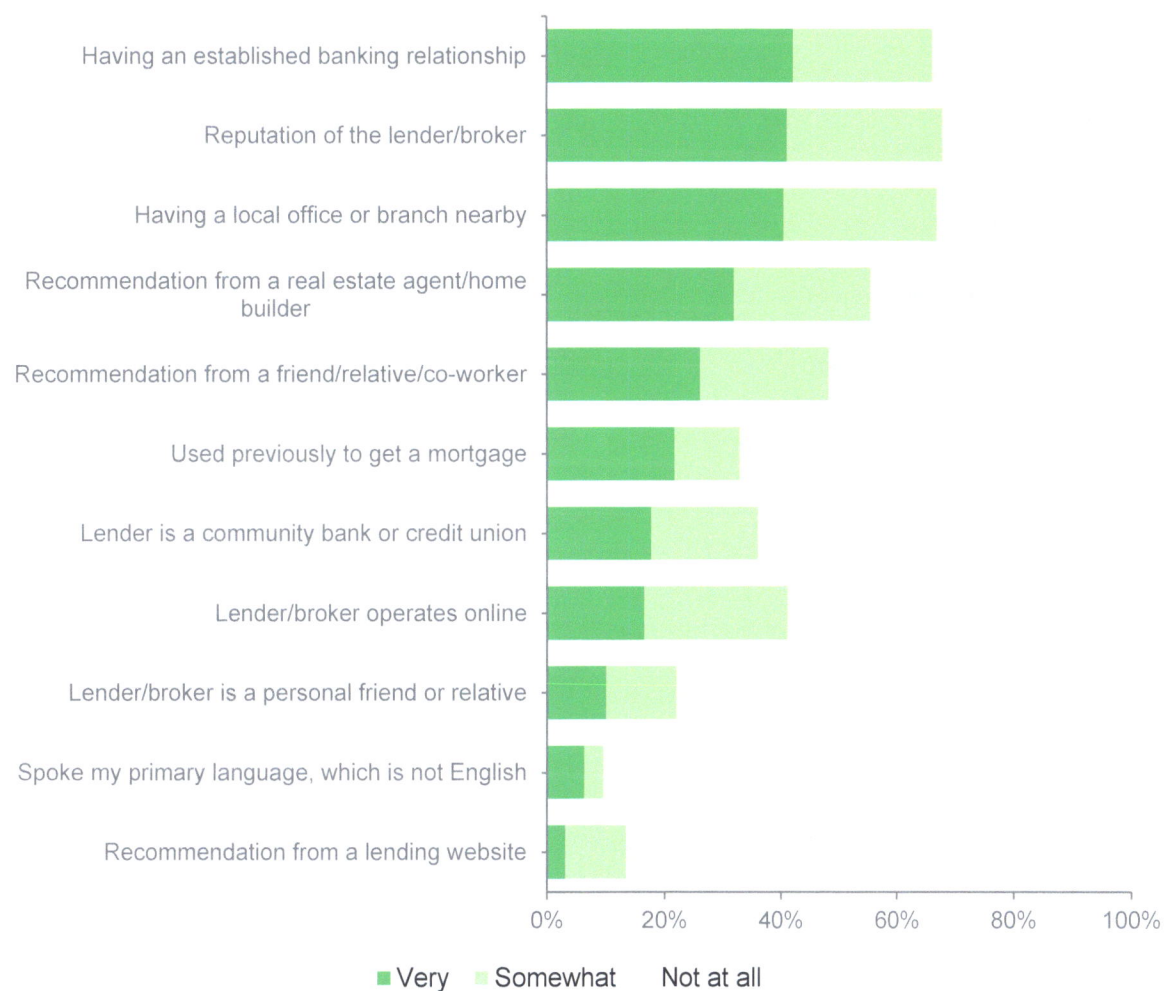

To better understand how such preferences may affect the extent of shopping, we calculate shopping intensity (again measured as the percentage of consumers who seriously considered multiple lenders before applying and whom we refer to as "shoppers") among consumers who indicated that each characteristic was "very important." Results are shown in Figure 14. For comparison, we also include the shopping intensity among borrowers who indicated that none of the characteristics was very important in their choice of lender or broker.

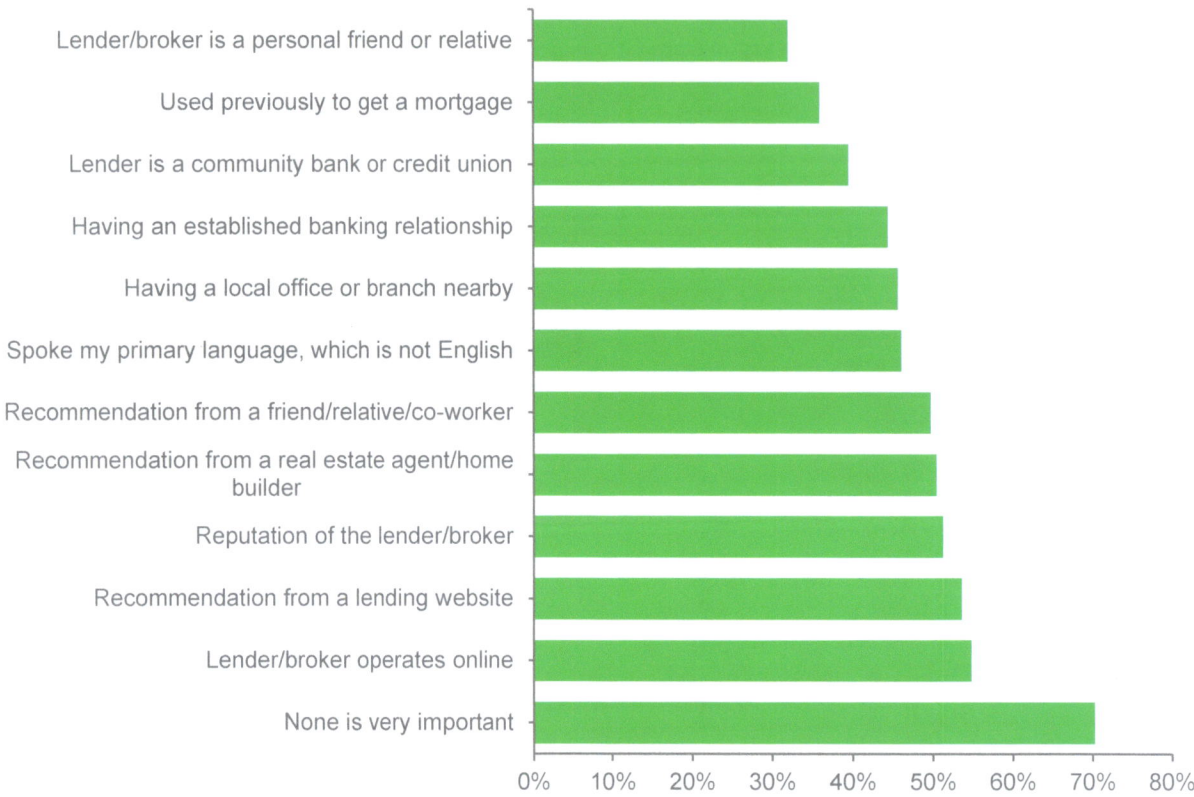

The results suggest that having a preference for one or more of these characteristics reduces the willingness to shop. Those consumers who indicated that none of the characteristics were very important to them were the most likely to shop (70 percent). In contrast, consumers were the least likely to shop if they considered it very important for the lender or broker to be a personal friend or relative. Consumers were also relatively less likely to shop if they felt it was very important that the lender be a community bank or credit union, be a lender or broker used previously to get a mortgage, or be someone with whom they have an established banking relationship. There are several potential explanations for why such preferences may inhibit shopping. Consumers may believe that such lenders provide the best deal for the consumers, feel loyalty to a bank or lender they have used in the past, or value the convenience of a local institution. Regardless of the reason, the effect of such non-monetary preferences is significant: Consumers who did not have a strong attachment to any of the listed characteristics were 40 percent more likely to shop than those who did. (See Figure 5.)

6. Conclusions

Buying a home is one of the most important financial decisions a consumer can make and selecting the mortgage that best meets the consumer's needs is an important part of that decision. As the recent crisis illustrated, mortgage features and pricing can have enormous impact on consumers' homeownership experiences. While many risky features are no longer permitted or available in the marketplace, mortgages still have different terms and features and consumers must be careful to select one that fits their needs and budget. For borrowers who know exactly what features of a mortgage they need, it may be possible to achieve substantial savings by shopping for a lower interest rate.

Our preliminary analysis of responses to the National Survey of Mortgage Borrowers reveals that consumers do not shop extensively for mortgages when purchasing a home. Instead, almost half of consumers who borrow to finance a home purchase only seriously consider a single lender or broker before choosing where to apply. While few consumers apply to more than one lender or broker, those who do are primarily motivated by a desire to get better loan terms suggesting that, at least for these consumers, shopping occurs throughout the mortgage process.

The primary source of information used by mortgage borrowers is their lender or broker, followed by their real estate agent. A smaller fraction of consumers obtains information from other sources that do not have a direct financial stake in the home purchase transaction and that may provide more unbiased information, such as websites, financial or housing counselors, or friends and relatives. While most mortgage borrowers report that they were very familiar with the mortgage process from the start, consumers with less familiarity appear to rely more heavily on real estate agents and personal acquaintances.

While these results provide interesting information about the shopping behavior of mortgage borrowers, they are preliminary and more work remains to be done. In particular, the current analysis has not attempted to evaluate the extent to which more shopping improves mortgage outcomes, such as better loan terms (e.g., lower interest rates, fewer points and fees) and fewer delinquencies and foreclosures.

The National Survey of Mortgage Borrowers, as part of the broader National Mortgage Database project being jointly developed by the CFPB and the Federal Housing Finance Agency, offers an opportunity to develop a much better understanding of consumer shopping behavior and how it affects mortgage outcomes. Going forward, research using these data will help inform policymakers and others about how mortgage markets are working for consumers.